Before You Sign an Apartment Lease

How Bad Landlords Get Away with Ripping Off Good Tenants – A Guide for Students, Parents, and Friends

By C. David Patterson

Table of Contents

How This Book About Bad Landlords Got Started

This book was written because an old friend reached out to me after his college-age daughter completed a lease with the Iowa City, Iowa-based company Apartments at Iowa, owned by a guy named Bryan James Clark. Clark also owns another rental company his father started, Apartments Downtown, as well as Apartments Near Campus.

My friend's daughter had gotten sick just prior to the start of a fall semester at the University of Iowa and had to withdraw. My friend attempted to sublet the apartment but encountered a lot of problems with the Apartments at Iowa rental office, especially with Megan Clabaugh, the property manager, and Chantrice Horne, the office manager, along with other staff. As time progressed, my friend reached out to additional players, such as the registered agent for the companies, attorneys C. Joseph Howell, who later retired, and his replacement, Erek P. Sittig.

The apartment ended up being subleased to somebody who, my friend later learned, was not subjected to a basic background check by the Apartments at Iowa rental office, despite an indication in the sublet agreement that this would be performed.

Even if the staff of Apartments at Iowa had spent a little time checking the subletter's name against the publicly available Iowa Courts web site, court records would have shown that the subletter had been legally evicted from another Iowa City apartment complex a couple years prior for non-payment of rent.

On this basis alone, the subletter should have been rejected. Other qualified applicants, and there were many, should have been considered. My friend later discovered that every major apartment rental company in the Iowa City area said they performed background checks on tenants, either primary lease holders or subletters.

In addition, the Apartments at Iowa rental office didn't require, per the sublet agreement, that the subletter post a deposit before letting the subletter move into the apartment, and then didn't inform my friend or his daughter that the subletter hadn't paid the required deposit.

The subletter never paid a penny in rent, and after a couple of months my friend contacted the Apartments at Iowa staff to get the subletter to pay something, or to be evicted. While the subletter was notified by the Apartments at Iowa staff, and the locks eventually changed, my friend later learned that the Apartments at Iowa staff had conducted an illegal eviction that violated Iowa law.

After the "eviction", my friend paid the rent current. At that time, he was told by Apartments at Iowa staff that he could seek an early termination of the lease. My friend was told that he just needed to talk to the property owner, but my friend didn't know the name of the owner at the time, although later this turned out to be Bryan James Clark.

My friend contacted the Registered Agent at the time (initially, attorney C. Joseph Holland, who was nearing retirement, and whose duties were taken over by attorney Erek P. Sittig). Over time, my friend realized that the owner, Bryan Clark, never had any intention of agreeing to an early termination of the lease even though the apartment was clean and ready for renting more than a month in advance of the start of spring semester.

After cleaning the filthy apartment, returning the subletter's stolen rental furniture to a couple of local companies, and figuring out that early termination of the lease would never be considered by the owner, my friend attempted to sublet the apartment for the spring semester, but the Apartments at Iowa rental office essentially ghosted him and refused to contact any potential subletters who inquired about the unit.

My friend filed a small claims lawsuit against Apartments at Iowa, but because the lease had not been completed, he ran into legal problems and had to withdraw the lawsuit. My friend ended up paying the entire lease, only to later get hit with phony cleaning fees, and other charges by Apartments at Iowa, when only part of the deposit was returned. Later, my friend learned that this is how the Clark family operates their apartment rental businesses, having been involved in a class action lawsuit about holding back deposit for phony cleaning fees and other matters that was settled in 2017.

As time progressed, my friend researched Apartments at Iowa, a sister company called Apartments Downtown, and the history of the Clark family's rental businesses. The whole situation became too overwhelming for him to think about, so he passed the story to me to further develop into this book.

Joseph and Loretta Clark started an apartment rental company in Iowa City in 1972, and it grew over time. Eventually their son Bryan took it over, although other family members and relatives were involved in various side businesses, family squabbles, and lengthy legal battles.

Around 2012, stories started appearing in the local news about lawsuits against the various Clark businesses. Student renters noticed that they had been charged for carpet cleaning when their apartment only contained hardwood floors. That's just the tip of the iceberg.

Considering the number of negative reviews on Yelp, Better Business Bureau, Google Reviews, and complaints on Reddit and other sites, my friend, and others, including this writer, seemed to agree that the rental companies owned by the Clarks appeared to be engaging in racketeering and theft on a massive scale against student renters over the decades.

Christopher Warnock, a local attorney who had fought against the Clarks in the past, got a class action lawsuit initiated about some of these cases. The class action lawsuit was settled by the Clarks in 2017, with each plaintiff receiving about $65 and some kind of "Housing Authority" process created - all of which we'll talk about later in this book.

My friend tried to reach out to local attorneys about whether he and his daughter had a case against Bryan James Clark. He also contacted local city council members, including Noah LeFevre and Matthew Monsivais, both UI Student Government liaisons, but heard nothing back.

Later, I discovered that one of the law firms my friend contacted and didn't hear back from, Phelan Tucker, had represented Bryan Clark and other family members in a lengthy court battle over a business partnership. In addition, the law firm that Registered Agent Erek P. Sittig worked for appears to have been acquired by Phelan Tucker. As of early 2024, Sittig works for Phelan Tucker and is still a Registered Agent for Bryan Clark.

After this, my friend called and talked to Warnock, a guy who does not look like a typical lawyer, has esoteric public interests outside of his profession, and whose web site looks like it hasn't been updated since 1997. That said, Warnock was the only person who talked with my friend and did so in a professional and respectful manner.

I won't reveal what Warnock advised to my friend. It seemed like good advice from the legal side, and I'll touch on it later in this book. I am not a lawyer, although I have been involved with many legal cases over the years.

Not long after talking with Warnock, my friend discussed with me what he and his daughter had been through.

I thought my friend's case would make an excellent short book on bad landlords, or perhaps a series of short books on the Clarks and their business practices.

My friend would never be able to put together a book on his own about this situation. Plus, he was so heavily involved. It was quite an ordeal for him and his daughter, but he agreed to show me the source material, knew that I loved research, was available for follow-up questions, and is grateful for the interest.

Based on the research so far, I have pitched other people on the idea of producing a documentary film on the Clarks and their rental businesses. We'll see if that gets made.

Will there be another lawsuit? It depends. My friend's daughter has up to 10 years after signing the original lease to file again, but she no longer lives in the Iowa City area. Lawsuits are a pain, take forever, and, as you'll see in this book, even if you "win" then the problem doesn't always get fixed in the long term.

Bad landlords and their staff know this, and that's how they exploit student renters.

So do the local politicians, media outlets, housing authority advocates, legal community, police, county prosecutors, and state attorney general's office.

As far as we're concerned, these all players are all worthless and self-serving if the bad landlords are allowed to continue doing business by scamming good tenants.

But you should know what could happen if you don't know what to look for in a potentially bad landlord.

This book will show you how to do some basic research to prevent signing a lease with a bad landlord.

About Online Reviews

One thing I noticed quickly in my research about Apartments at Iowa and Apartments Downtown were all the 1-star reviews on Google Reviews, Yelp, and the Better Business Bureau web site, and a lot of negative comments on Reddit.

How do people not see these negative reviews and heed their warnings?

If a bad landlord gets that many bad reviews, how can they stay in business?

That's because most online reviews have little influence.

Or people don't see it.

They didn't think about doing any research on the property management company.

Maybe they knew somebody who lived at the apartment complex and was assured that everything was fine.

Or they took a tour of an apartment. Gee, the guide was friendly. Everything can be handled online. And the price is lower compared to the other apartments.

Most negative reviews aren't that lengthy, or they're poorly written.

Some of the negative reviews seem like they were written by bad tenants.

I'm sure a lot of the tenants of Apartments at Iowa, Apartments Downtown, and Apartments Near Campus had a perfectly acceptable situation. But they don't write about it.

Some reviews disappear over time. If the bad landlord changes the name of their company, which the Clarks have done in the past, then that record of negative reviews either disappears or becomes lost.

I'm not criticizing people who fail to heed the obvious warnings, but I'm afraid I must mention this glaring oversight on the part of potential tenants.

And if a bad landlord has a reputation with scores and scores of negative reviews, why do the local politicians, legal community, media, housing authority, activists, and others not call the landlord out for their behavior?

This book is to teach you how to do additional research before signing a lease – whether it's for yourself, a friend, or a relative.

How a Bad Landlord Rips Off Tenants

Once you sign a lease, a bad landlord can do whatever they want.

A bad landlord can instruct their maintenance staff to be on the lookout during the year for anything they can dock your deposit on after moving out, such as broken plastic louvers on old window shades or fake crumbs in the oven.

When they're bringing future prospective tenants through, you can be sure that the office staff are on the lookout for cleaning issues and taking notes.

If the bad landlord's staff aren't looking for ways to take your deposit, some employees or contracted staff who are in your apartment might be looking to steal things.

If you can't be in your apartment, always keep anything of value hidden or locked away. And have a clandestine, motion-activated camera running.

If landlord staff have been in your apartment, always check afterwards to make sure the windows are closed and locked.

Does the apartment's hallway and exterior have "security cameras"? Do you know if they work? Are you sure they aren't being used to monitor when the tenants are away? The bad landlord might use "security cameras" for nefarious purposes.

At the end of your lease, after you've thoroughly cleaned your apartment, taken photos in portrait mode with good lighting at different lengths, and gone through an extensive checklist of items you might get dinged on, such as light bulbs or the cleanliness of the oven, the bad landlord could just make things up to take away part of the deposit.

If you get your deposit back a month after moving out, and you've been charged $300 dollars for "cleaning" and various repairs that you know are fraudulent, then what are you going to do?

If you call the bad landlord's office, they will blame you and probably laugh after you hang up. They know they have the upper hand.

At that point, you'll want to file a small claims lawsuit.

As of 2024, in Johnson County, Iowa, if you're suing a bad landlord like Apartments at Iowa or Apartments Downtown, it costs $95 to file.

You must still be living in the area, otherwise you'll have to travel to deal with the case.

After filing a small claim lawsuit in Iowa, you are required to attend "mediation" first, which is a joke and a waste of time, and we'll talk about that later.

You must know how to use the confusing computer system provided by the court to upload exhibits.

You also need to know how to build a case.

If you've never done any of that before, you will have trouble because the bad landlord usually has an attorney ready to fight you, even in small claims court, and even if the landlord is wrong.

And if the landlord loses, even in small claims court, they will appeal.

What the Tenant Doesn't Know

Who are the people working for the landlord? Do you know their full names?

Who is the property manager? Are there multiple property managers? Is there an office manager? Is there a maintenance manager?

What is the background of the landlord's management staff? Have any of them been sued before? Have any been legally evicted by court order? You might not be dealing with law-abiding people.

Does the landlord's web site have pictures of their employees and their names?

If you call the office, or stop by, do the people working for the landlord refuse to give their last names?

Do you know who the owner of the apartment building is? How do you look that up? (I'll show you in the next chapter)

Has the owner been involved in lawsuits over the years as a defendant? Are they mentioned in the local newspaper?

Is there a picture of the owner anywhere? Google Images? Newspaper archive search? Have you called the local newspaper and asked if they have a photo of the owner on file?

What's a Registered Agent and what do they do?

Look at how complicated this has become.

If you can't easily answer most of these questions when considering an apartment lease, then you need to educate yourself before signing a lease.

What Are Business Entities, Registered Agents, and the Biennial Report

Business Entities:

Landlords almost always operate their rental business as some kind of corporation, usually a limited liability corporation or LLC. This is normal.

Most companies, especially if they are local people, establish their LLC in the state where they reside.

For this example, we'll use the State of Iowa.

Business entities can be discovered on the Secretary of State's web site. In the case of Apartments at Iowa, located in Iowa City, Iowa, you can search for the business entity name.

At the time of writing this book, in 2024, I can see the Business Entity Summary on the Iowa Secretary of State's web site. The business number is 443475 and has the legal name of APARTMENTS AT IOWA LC. It is a Code 489 Domestic Limited Liability Company.

The Registered Agent is Erek P Sittig of 321 E Market St, PO Box 2150, Iowa City, IA 52244, which is the address of the Phelan Tucker law firm, where Sittig worked in 2024.

Home Office is listed as 355 S Gilbert St, Iowa City, IA 52240, which is the landlord office of Apartments at Iowa.

But my friend's lease said something else. The lease was with a company called 1000 LLC, not Apartments at Iowa.

If I enter 1000 LLC into the Business Entities Search, I can see the Business Entity Summary. The business number is 417779 and has a legal name of 1000 LLC, and it's a Code 489 Domestic Limited Liability Company.

The registered agent is Erek P Sittig, same as Apartments at Iowa Lc, but the Home Office is showing as 414 E Market

St, Iowa City, IA 52245. 414 E Market St is the landlord office of Apartments Downtown, a separate company owned by the same people.

See how it can get confusing?

Say you sign a lease with Apartments at Iowa, but the lease says 1000 LLC. If you have problems with the landlord and file a lawsuit against Apartments at Iowa, it could be initially rejected by the defendant because you should be suing 1000 LLC.

It's the little things like this that you must be aware of before signing a lease, much less filing a lawsuit.

The lawyers for bad landlords know all about these kinds of details.

I hope you're not thinking that lawyers are ethical people who are concerned about "the law", like on some stupid TV show or movie. I'm sure a few out there are Perry Mason or Atticus Finch, but too many lawyers are degenerates just trying to create some billable hours. They could care less about what's right or ethical.

What is a Registered Agent?

A registered agent is an individual (or business) designated to receive legal matters when a company is getting sued. This is also known as "receiving service of process".

If the registered agent is an attorney, chances are the business entity deals with a lot of lawsuits. This doesn't mean the business is crooked. To be fair, being a landlord is not easy, especially in a small town with a big university. Even the occasional screened tenant can turn out to be a loser who needs to be sued or evicted. But the bad landlords will use their registered agent attorney as a defense strategy even if the landlord and the apartment management staff are in the wrong.

For most non-landlord small businesses, the registered agent is the same as the owner. You can confirm this by looking at the Biennial Report on business entity search results of the Secretary of State's web site, which I'll get to in a little bit.

It helps to do some research on the registered agent if they're an attorney. What is their past work history? Have they ever been a 2-star, hearse-chaser working out of a sleazy strip mall? Or are they a lawyer who sits on the back bench, drifting from law firm to law firm, and unable to become a partner in the firm? These kinds of lawyers might have no ethical problem working for the bad guys.

The Biennial Report

On Iowa's Business Entity Summary, there are a bunch of subcategories: address, agent, filings, names, officers, stock, and protected series.

The best place to look is Filings. Any Active business entity is required by law to file a biennial (every two years) report, or the business entity will be deemed inactive.

For example, 1000 LLC has a certificate of organization filed on May 26, 2011. Every two years, a biennial report is filed.

Until December 2, 2022, the registered agent for 1000 LLC was C. Joseph Holland, an attorney. After December 2, 2022, it changed to Erek P Sittig, an attorney. On August 24, 2023, Mr. Sittig's work address changed to the law offices of Phelan Tucker, 321 E. Market Street, PO Box 2150, Iowa City, IA 52244.

Also listed on the biennial report is the owner, Bryan James Clark.

How to Use Your Library Card to Find Reference Information

Now that you know how to look up a business entity filing, and know what a Registered Agent is and does, and how to find the actual name of the building owner, it's time to dig up the dirt.

Most libraries have an online reference section where you can access things like the Newspaper Archive, or a digital archive of local newspapers, like the Iowa City Press-Citizen.

If you live outside of the Iowa City area, you might not have access to the Press-Citizen archive, but there are ways to obtain access. Your local library might have access through various sites. If you're in Iowa, the State Library of Iowa might have access. And the University of Iowa's Daily Iowan student newspaper does have an online archive, although it's difficult to effectively search.

Finally, if you're visiting Iowa City and don't have a library card, you can always do research within the Iowa City Public Library on the 2nd floor.

Keyword searching is a good start. If you wanted to research Bryan Clark, you would likely want to put his name in quotes: "Bryan Clark" or "Bryan James Clark", or the name of his businesses, "Apartments at Iowa" or "Apartments Downtown", or any prior names discovered on the Secretary of State's web site.

Any major lawsuits will make the newspaper.

Just because a landlord is involved in a lawsuit doesn't make them bad, or guilty.

But, in the case of Bryan James Clark, if you repeatedly see his name and business entity names in the paper over the decades and involved in questionable business practices such as withholding deposits for carpet cleaning when the apartment only had hardwood floors, it's time to look for a different apartment to rent.

How to Search Public Court Records

Iowa has had an excellent and free online court search since the 1990s.

Learning how to use it effectively is not easy. Landlords, especially, are often involved with lawsuits as a plaintiff against bad renters or squatters.

You just need to understand how to search for the landlord or business entity as a defendant.

Some law firms and legal sites may post public records about cases. This can be discovered via Google or Bing. That's how I was able to find details about the Lillie Christophersen case, which you'll read about later.

Why Your Friends Give Bad Advice

If your college-age kid has problems with their bad landlord, what are you going to do?

Your friends might say to talk to a local lawyer.

That's usually a bad idea. Most lawyers in smaller, college-dominated towns went to school together or are members of the same country club.

There's a good chance the lawyer you're talking to might have been involved in other cases involving the bad landlord. How do you know without major research?

Don't bother with trying to piece things together on social media sites like Facebook or LinkedIn. A lot of lawyers smartly avoid those sites.

Even the lawyers who have fought and won against a bad landlord might be little more than an actor towards you. They can play you for the fool while logrolling with the other side to pull down some hefty representation fees.

Trust nobody, especially lawyers.

Your friends might say to talk to the local housing authority.

What sort of "authority" does anybody on a "housing authority" board really have?

These losers are like the clowns who served in student government in grade school.

They do nothing except virtue signal to others about how they're on the "housing authority".

Or they get quoted in the newspaper about how they're trying to help "marginalized people".

It's all bullshit. They're nothing but self-described "activists" who have done nothing but pad their resume. Avoid any "housing authority" people.

Your friends might say to talk to somebody at the university.

The college or university could care less about your situation. All they want is your tuition money now and, later in life, some alumni money.

Don't waste your time with these assholes.

It wasn't that long ago when the Iowa Hawkeyes' football and basketball coaches, the Athletic Director, the Dean of Students, and others were trying to internally adjudicate rape and sexual assault cases involving student-athletes as defendants.

What do you think your odds are with getting any justice through the university system? Absolutely zero. If the university has little to no concern for rape and sexual assault victims – not just accusers but actual victims – then your case involving a bad landlord will fall on deaf ears and be a complete waste of time.

How about the cops?

Absolutely not. You have a "civil matter", not a criminal matter. The cops will say this even if the landlord's staff is breaking into your apartment and stealing the microwave. Anyway, it's impossible to prove who stole the microwave.

What about the local county attorney?

That's always a bad idea. 98% of what a county attorney does is to make a deal with actual criminals with track records a mile long. The last thing a county attorney's office wants to do is any real work.

Why Lawsuits Are a Bad Idea

At this point, I'm going to sound like I'm repeating myself, but I must say this again so that you understand how difficult filing a lawsuit can be:

1. Have you ever filed a small claims lawsuit?

2. How much is the filing fee?

3. Do you know how to perform service of the lawsuit to the defendant and what it costs?

4. Did you fill out everything correctly on the court's confusing, 1997-style web site? If not, the Clerk of Court will soon reject you.

5. What is the legal argument for your case?

6. Do you have all your Exhibits ready and ordered and in PDF format?

7. Do you have all the photos or video ready?

8. Can you explain your case in just a few minutes?

9. Can you anticipate everything that the defendant will try to do to wear you down or get the case delayed or dismissed?

10. Even if you win in small claims, did you know the lawsuit can be appealed?

11. If you win, what do you have to do if the defendant doesn't pay the judgment?

If you can't answer most of those questions without looking up the answers on the internet, you're not ready to file a small claims lawsuit.

As for amounts higher than the small claims limit in your state, navigating that world requires an attorney, and they aren't cheap.

In Iowa, if you file a small claims lawsuit, you will first be required to attend "mediation". Mediation is meeting between the plaintiff and defendant and is usually coordinated by somebody who pretends to be a mediator.

The defendant does not have to show up for mediation, and there is no penalty except having your time wasted.

In my friend's case, the defendant didn't show up for mediation. The property manager, Megan Clabaugh, and her sidekick, office manager Chantrice Horne, and some female bookkeeper, showed up and filibustered the proceedings. They had no intention of making a settlement.

This is by design.

It's part of the bad landlord's legal strategy.

This is how Bryan James Clark operates.

Notice how the registered agent, attorney Erek P. Sittig, didn't attend the mediation.

Clark and Sittig, as well as Clabaugh and Horne, had absolutely no intention of settling anything.

Once meditation fails, you immediately go before a judge, and they set a trial date.

Along the way, the attorney for the bad landlord may file motions to delay the trial.

Do you have any experience dealing with legal motions?

Small claims court wasn't supposed to be about complicated legal filings, but that's how it has evolved.

Who evolved it? Lawyers, of course. Asshole lawyers.

Why the Media is Completely Worthless

Maybe you could just let the media know about your landlord issue: the newspapers, the alternative weekly, and the TV stations. Don't they want a hot scoop on a crooked evildoer?

Absolutely not!

The people working in "journalism" these days are the most obedient losers who will defend the crooked establishment.

Corporate newspapers are the worst.

The Iowa City Press-Citizen is owned by Gannett, which is further owned by some foreign conglomerate. Does the

Press-Citizen even have an office in Iowa City anymore?
Has anybody with a byline at that paper lived in Iowa City
for any length of time? Do they know the history of the
city, and the players in town, or even care?

And who reads the newspaper these days? Old people
looking at obituaries. Maybe somebody at the doctor's
office. That's it. Nobody cares. Most of the content of
newspapers is inert nonsense written by robots.

Isn't there a student-run newspaper at the University of
Iowa? Yes, it's called the Daily Iowan, or its nickname, the
Daily Idiot. Nobody reads it. The newspaper has zero
influence on the community. It is worse than a high school
newspaper.

What about the weekly "alternative" paper? Iowa City has
something called Little Village, which has "core values" of
"economic and labor justice", "critical culture", and all the
other empty leftist slogans. I'm sure the local "housing
authority" members are quoted often.

Rags like the Little Village could care less if you handed
them the scoop of the century that checked off all their
boxes because you're not in their clique.

Even if you do convince them to write an article, nobody will read it, and nothing will happen. No local lawyer or politician is going to step up and take your case.

Doesn't one of the local TV stations have a "call for action" reporter named Stan or Dick who advocates for the little guy? No, those guys retired, died, or were fired for hitting on the young female reporters. Those days are over. Today, all local TV stations look the same and few have any actual reporters looking out for the little guy.

If you don't believe me, go take your story to any of these media outlets and see what happens. It will be ignored. The media outlet can't afford to upset an apartment rental company that might advertise with them, or their wealthy friends. That's how the world works today.

At worst, you'll make yourself a target of the media if the landlord, or their friends, do any advertising with the media outlet. That's how "journalism" happens these days.

Just like with cops, never talk to "journalists". Don't do it! You will regret it. At least the cop will tell you that he can't help because it's a civil matter, which is true. The "journalist" will spend time digging through your past Tweets and Facebook posts, looking for the time when you were 13 years old and decided to quote some Drake lyrics.

If you don't believe me, find out what happened to Carson King, a University of Iowa student who wanted to establish a charity for the Children's Hospital in Iowa City. King got trashed in the media by Aaron Calvin, an asshole "reporter" at the awful and evil Des Moines Register, who went through King's high school-era tweets that nobody saw or remembered and make an example of him because King quoted some rap lyrics.

My point is: nobody should make themselves a target of the modern-day terrorist media. Don't go to the media with your problems, however right you are.

What I Would Have Advised My Friend and His Daughter

It's easy to say that my friend and his daughter should have taken more care before she signed that lease and then became sick and had to withdraw from school.

My friend learned everything over time, and along the way. It wasn't like he had all the answers at any point until the end. He relied on people in the apartment rental office to be straight shooters, but they weren't. They were liars. They withheld information. They later doctored papers that attorney Erek P. Sittig uploaded as defense exhibits.

I know a lot of people would insert a disclaimer now saying, "I'm not a lawyer and this isn't legal advice", as if lawyers are somehow moral people who give a shit about the law. Most aren't trustworthy. If you're an attorney and your ego can't handle me saying this, maybe you should spend some time trying to clean up your filthy profession.

Here's the advice I would have given to my friend at the various stages:

Is the subletter refusing to pay rent? Don't pay the rent current, which my friend didn't do, and was the right thing to do.

What do you do after the subletter is removed? Clean the apartment. If there's stolen rental furniture, like my friend discovered, find out who owns it and have the company retrieve it. Do not pay the rent current, something my friend did do after cleaning the apartment. It was a huge mistake because he was misled by the Apartments at Iowa rental office staff.

Try to negotiate an early termination of the lease. While I hate lawyers, I think this might be a good time to throw $200 at one so they can send a letter asking about negotiating an early termination of the lease. Pick an annoying local "activist" lawyer for this kind of work. Ask the local "housing authority" members or weekly tabloid editor for recommendations. It could be money down the drain, and the bad landlord might not respond, but at this point you've already got "sunk costs" happening. It will show good faith to the judge if the landlord decides to file for eviction or sue to recover unpaid rent.

What if the landlord threatens to sue? They won't, at first. They'll send it to a collections agency who will harass you.

Make sure nobody from the apartment management company or the landlord is entering the empty apartment because it's likely they will pull shenanigans and intentionally cause problems. Examples would be: breaking plastic louvers on window shades, stealing the microwave oven, jacking the thermostat up in the winter and then cracking a window, or taking a shit and not flushing. The lease typically requires notice before landlord staff can enter the unit on an occasional basis.

What is the first legal thing the landlord will do? If the landlord won't respond to the early termination request from another lawyer, wait for the landlord to file for eviction.

In my friend's case, for the squatting subletter, the Apartments at Iowa property management office did not file what's known as a "forcible entry and detainer" (FED) as part of Chapter 648 of the Iowa Code on the subletter.

My friend believes this is because either Megan Clabaugh and/or Chantrice Horne didn't deem the subletter as a "legal tenant", possibly because the subletter didn't pay a deposit before moving in. My friend has paperwork showing the subletter as approved by Apartments at Iowa and was allowed to move in, and one of the requirements in the paperwork was that the subletter had to first pay a deposit. This matter probably would have been noticed by a judge at the hearing for a FED if my friend's daughter had been served. I can't say this for certain. My friend didn't realize that the "eviction" of the subletter was completely illegal until many months later.

This is especially ironic because Chantrice Horne should know all about Chapter 648 FEDs, as she has been served one in the past and was evicted for non-payment of rent a few years before she started working for Bryan James Clark with Apartments at Iowa. It's in the Iowa Court Search web site for all to see.

Megan Clabaugh, C. Joseph Howell, Erek P Sittig, and Bryan James Clark, of all people, should know how FEDs work. They have filed or been involved with many FEDs and evictions over the years when bad tenants didn't pay their rent. Again, this can be found in the Iowa Court Search public records.

Why wasn't a FED filed on my friend's squatting subletter? Because Megan Clabaugh and/or Chantrice Horne think they can get away with anything. They can justify saying the subletter isn't a legal tenant because of their mistake, whether on purpose or not, and then not informing my friend and his daughter. Megan Clabaugh and/or Chantrice Horne think they are judge and jury, because they can operate that way with impunity. It's like the way that attorney Erek P. Sittig acts as the enforcer of whatever Bryan James Clark wants to get away with. These assholes act outside of the law and get away with it because they've gotten away with it for most of their careers.

What are the most important things to do? Don't pay the landlord any money. Try to negotiate.

Buy as much time as possible. My friend and his daughter knew little along the way. Once they got to court, and attorney Erek P Sittig filed the defendant's exhibits, this was when my friend discovered the extent of the corruption and deception on the part of the Apartments at Iowa rental office. If my friend had been on the defense, it would have been easier for him to point these things out to the judge and get the original lease terminated in court.

Finally, don't directly negotiate with any of these people. If you think you're dealing with idiots, crooks, or scumbags, or you later discover their sordid history, cut off all talk. Don't call. Don't send them letters. Spend as little as possible to have a local attorney communicate with them. You don't have to hire an attorney on retainer, as if for a case. You can hire an attorney simply as an advisor, or to send letters, which is much cheaper.

Why the Politicians Hide

You'd think with scores of 1-star reviews all over the internet, years of being in and out of the newspaper with negative story after negative story, and then settling a class action lawsuit with plaintiffs, that landlords like Bryan James Clark in Iowa City would be put on notice and made an example of by the politicians.

It didn't happen. Nothing happened! What gives?

All the elected politicians in the Iowa City area are Democrats. That's part of the problem.

But haven't we been told forever that the Democrats are here to help the "little guy"?

Democrats do not care about the little guy!

Neither do the Republicans, but the Democrats have nothing but contempt for the bourgeoisie, the middle classes.

I don't know the politics of people like Bryan James Clark or his family, but if you can safely get away with screwing over lots of good tenants for over 15 years, then why are the local Democrat politicians seemingly giving Clark a wink and nod to continue to do "business as usual" in his usual crooked ways?

Erek Sittig, the registered agent and attorney for Clark, was elected to the North Liberty City Council. His campaign propaganda said he was running for a city council seat "to help the downtrodden". Is that supposed to be a joke? Sittig was the attorney who lost twice in small claims court against Lillie Christophersen, a case you'll read about in a little bit.

Why don't politicians, especially Democrat politicians, try to stop the bad landlords?

Because politicians are lazy.

Politicians like to cause problems and chaos because it empowers them.

If a politician can choose between a bad idea that helps

them and a good idea that helps regular people, politicians will always choose the bad idea that helps them.

So why would the politicians in the Iowa City area even care about whether student renters are being screwed over? The politicians don't because the students don't have any money. Students are usually transitory residents, and young, and broke. Besides, the community has a "housing authority", so it's likely the lazy politicians assume that "fairness" is being handled there.

Why Tenants Who Have Been Ripped Off Don't Want to Talk About It

When researching this book, I discovered some people who didn't want to talk about their experience with Apartments at Iowa and Apartments Downtown.

Some found it difficult. It dredged up bad feelings. They've taken it on the chin and moved on. They realized they messed up by signing a lease with a rotten company and couldn't fight back. They were warned by others, but signed the lease anyway, and getting ripped off at the end is the "how things are done".

Many would talk on Reddit, but anonymously. If Reddit or the Internet Archive are out there, you can read what others have written. But the internet always seems temporary, whereas a book seems like a more permanent record.

How to Organize in the Age of the Internet

I know a lot of people used to create Facebook groups, but Facebook is unreliable.

Reddit can be a good place to vent, but I feel that Reddit won't last forever, or it'll get wiped or censored.

TikTok, in 2024, seems to be a way to talk about topics. Like everything else, it's a matter of time before these sites go away.

Mailing lists and blogs can be buried out of the public eye but are also good ways to organize in the shorter term.

Nobody wants to admit they've been had.

Too many people believe the court system exists to help the little guy. It does not! It is designed by lawyers – for lawyers!

After hearing my friend's story, and seeing the paperwork, I think publishing a series of books about Bryan James Clark, his father, who goes by different first names, and the various lawsuits they've been involved with over the years is a great way to shine a light on what's going on.

The books may not make a big splash at first, but over time they should have some impact.

Another thing is the idea of a documentary film on the Clarks and their business practices. That is likely happening down the road. Today, it's so easy to provide a basic documentary quickly and cheaply. It doesn't have to be a feature-length movie shown in a theater. It just needs a compelling story, and we think the story of the Clarks in Iowa City is worthy of telling.

Case Study: Lillie Christophersen vs. Apartments Downtown

Let's move on and present the Lillie Christophersen case.

Lillie's case is important because it demonstrates what a bunch of assholes the Clarks are, along with their attorney, Erek P. Sittig. It also shows what a nightmare fighting them in court can be.

Any reasonable landlord would have settled with the tenant and would not have retaliated in such a manner with defending the lawsuit, much less appealing it.

The court record does not indicate the name of the property manager that Christophersen had to deal with at the Apartments Downtown.

CASE No.: 06521 SCSC092479, in the Iowa District Court for Johnson County.

The Court finds the following facts.

The Plaintiff, Lillie Christophersen, signed a lease with Apartments Downtown for a rental until at 108 S. Linn Street, Unit 27. When Ms. Christophersen proceeded to move into the apartment on August 4, 2017, she found live and dead cockroaches throughout the apartment. There were live cockroaches in plain sight as well as hiding behind appliances and in the cabinets.

Mr. Christophersen, Lillie's father, credibly testified that he saw live cockroaches scurry away before he was able to take a picture of them. The Plaintiff did provide pictures of the condition of the apartment with pictures of both alive and dead cockroaches. There was also evidence of cockroach fecal matter and moltings of cockroach exoskeletons. The fecal matter and exoskeletons were also found in the cabinetry, behind appliances, and otherwise on the floor.

The Court further finds that the Plaintiff immediately gave notice to the landlord of the problem as well as her intent to terminate the lease because the apartment was unfit and uninhabitable. The problem was not fixed within 5 days. The Plaintiff alleged finding cockroaches of approximately 20 or 30 in broad daylight and in bait traps.

The city inspector for Iowa City, Mr. Tage, credibly testified that he found numerous dead and alive cockroaches in the apartment in November 2017. The Court does not believe the testimony from Mr. Mattson that there were no cockroaches present on his visit in October 2017. Mr. Mattson testified that he spent a short time reviewing the apartment. He also indicated he reviewed the other areas with cockroaches in the building.

The Court believes the infestation continued from August 2017 through January 2018 when the City Inspector approved the rental permit following a clean inspection.

The Court notes that the Plaintiff's did not request attorney fees, so no fees are ordered. The Court believes that was appropriate in this case as the Defendant appears to have taken its obligation to contain the pest problem seriously.

The Defendant has hired a reputable pest control company and has them routinely spray and provide other treatments for various pests and bugs. However, in the Court's view the evidence established that bugs are difficult to control. A landlord may take reasonable steps to prevent an infestation and that may not prevent the problem in all situations. The amount of cockroaches present in plain sight and caught in traps sufficiently proves to the Court that there were a lot more hiding in the walls and other locations in the apartment. This level of cockroach infestation made the apartment unfit and uninhabitable as those terms are used in the Landlord and Tenant Act.

The Court believes the testimony of Mr. Mattson that hundreds of cockroaches can be a health hazard. The health issue includes both airborne issues as well as spreading germs such as E.Coli and Salmanella. Mr. Mattson also testified that 20 or 30 cockroaches running around could be a health problem. It depends what they are getting in to. He further testified that seeing cockroaches in the open during broad daylight could be a sign that they were pushed out based on overcrowding in their hiding places.

The Court finds that the Plaintiff proved by a preponderance of the evidence the apartment was unfit and uninhabitable when she gave notice to the landlord. The Court further finds the notice was received and the lease was appropriately terminated after five days pursuant to Iowa Code Section 562A.22. Bond on appeal is $3,000.00.

What did Bryan James Clark of Apartments Downtown do after losing the case in small claims court?

Clark ordered attorney Erek P. Sittig to appeal his loss, which is his right, but it's the kind of move only a dickhead would make.

Order on Appeal

Case No SCSC092479 in the Iowa District Court in and for Johnson County. Lillie Christophersen v. Apartments Downtown and Apartments Near Campus.

This matter comes before the Court on Defendants' appeal from the judgment order entered on August 29, 2018 by Magistrate David Cox. The Notice of Appeal was filed on September 17, 2018 and, pursuant to a scheduling order establish by Judge Miller, the Defendant/Appellant filed their appeal argument on November 11, 2018 and the Plaintiff/Appellee filed their brief on November 22, 2018. The Court has reviewed the record, the arguments on appeal, and the relevant law and now enters the following order.

STATEMENT OF FACTS AND PROCEDURE The magistrate found the following facts in the original judgment: The Plaintiff, Lillie Christophersen, signed a lease with Apartments Downtown for a rental until [sic] at 108 S. Linn Street, Unit 27. When Ms. Christophersen proceeded to move into the apartment on August 4, 2017, she found live and dead cockroaches throughout the apartment. There were live cockroaches in plain sight as well as hiding behind appliances and in the cabinets. Mr. Christophersen, Lillie's father, credibly testified that he saw live cockroaches scurry away before he was able to take a picture of them. The Plaintiff did provide pictures of the condition of the apartment with pictures of both alive and dead cockroaches. There was also evidence of cockroach fecal matter and moltings [sic] of cockroach exoskeletons. The fecal matter and exoskeletons were also found in the cabinetry, behind appliances, and otherwise on the floor. The Court further finds that the Plaintiff immediately gave notice to the landlord of the problem as well as her intent to terminate the lease because the apartment was unfit and uninhabitable. The problem was not fixed within 5 days. The Plaintiff alleged finding cockroaches of approximately 20 or 30 in broad daylight and in bait traps. The city inspector for Iowa City, Mr. Tage [sic], credibly testified that he found numerous dead and alive cockroaches in the apartment in November 2017. The Court does not believe the testimony from Mr. Mattson that there were no cockroaches present on his visit in October 2017. Mr. Mattson testified that he spent a short time reviewing the apartment. He also indicated he reviewed the other areas with cockroaches in the building. The Court believes the infestation continued from August 2017 through January 2018 when the City Inspector approved the rental permit following a clean inspection. Judgment Order, August 29, 2018. The Magistrate found that the apartment was unfit and uninhabitable when Plaintiff gave notice to the landlord and that the lease was appropriately terminated within five days, pursuant to Iowa Code section 562A.22. Id. The Appellant states in its appeal brief that Ms. Christophersen paid $2,010 upon signing her lease, to cover a $300 security deposit and the first and last month's rent of $855 per month. That $2,010 is the only damages in dispute in this case. She stated on taking possession of the unit that she would not rent it because of a cockroach infestation, which created an uninhabitable and unhealthy environment, pursuant to Iowa Code section 562A.22. The Appellant in large part challenges the use of the term "infestation" by the city housing inspector, where Mr. Tatge, the inspector, never saw a live cockroach in that unit. According to the City code, an infestation requires a number of insects that creates unsanitary conditions. The Appellant's expert, the Branch Manager for Orkin Pest Control in Cedar Rapids, defined an infestation as requiring the presence of all states of an insect's life cycle at the same time. Additionally, large numbers can constitute an infestation, but the evidence of Ms. Christophersen's unit did not demonstrate the requisite number. Additionally, he states that Apts. Downtown was aware of the problem and was taking steps to manage it. Generally, the Appellant argues that the condition of the apartment unit was not so bad as to violate the implied warrant of habitability or violate the applicable building and housing courts for health and safety. The Appellee states in her appeal brief that the evidence presented was sufficient to support the trial court's conclusion that the residence was uninhabitable and unhealthy due to cockroach infestation. The Appellee emphasizes that even Appellant's expert admitted based on his company's website that even 20-30 cockroaches could be a health problem. Trial Transcript at 43. The Appellee relies on the Iowa Uniform Residential Landlord Tenant Act ("IURLTA") and the Iowa City Municipal Code to establish the standards of habitability. Establishing the warrantee of habitability, the Appellee goes on to cite the Municipal Code's definition of "infestation": "The presence, within or around a dwelling, of any insects, rodents or other pests in such quantities as would be considered unsanitary." Iowa City Municipal Code 17-5-3. Appellee then provides case law to support her argument that a pest infestation is sufficient to make the unity unsanitary and unfit in violation of the warrant of habitability. The Court found that the Plaintiff had met her burden by a preponderance of the evidence, but the Appellee notes that as to the security deposit, the burden was on the landlord to provide proof. Iowa Code § 562A.12(3)(b).

STANDARD OF REVIEW This Court hears an appeal from a small claims decision upon the record filed without further evidence. Iowa Code § 631.13(4) (2017). The appeal is a de novo review of the record. Sunset Mobile Home Park v. Parsons, 324 N.W.2d 452, 454 (Iowa 1982). The Court gives weight to the fact findings of the trial court, especially when considering the credibility of witnesses, but is not bound by them. Jack Moritz Co. Management v.

Walker, 429 N.W.2d 127, 128 (Iowa 1988). This Court, after examining the court file and the record made by Magistrate Cynthia Finley, finds such record adequate for rendering a final judgment on appeal. DISCUSSION The question on appeal is not whether there were cockroaches in Ms. Christophersen's apartment, but whether there were sufficient cockroaches so as to constitute an infestation that made the apartment unfit and uninhabitable, such that Ms. Christophersen was justified in terminating her tenancy under Iowa Code section 562A.22. Although the Appellant's expert has attempted to define infestation according to the insect stages present, for the purposes of this proceeding the Court will rely on the definition contained in the Iowa City Municipal Code on Housing. There "infestation" is defined as "the presence, within or around a dwelling, of any insects, rodents or other pests in such quantities as would be considered unsanitary." Iowa Municipal Code 17-5-3. Therefore, the question before the Court is whether the quantity present in Ms. Christophersen's apartment "would be considered unsanitary." It is not enough to say that an infestation of insects is unsanitary, as many of the cases cited by the Appellee appear to do. That would be circular in that infestation is defined by the quantity that would be considered unsanitary. Without getting caught in the terminology, the question remains whether the quantity of cockroaches present was unsanitary, and thus in breach of the warrant of habitability. On this issue, the Appellee presented the testimony of the city inspector at trial and the Appellant presented the testimony of a pest control manager from Orkin Pest Control Services in Cedar

Rapids. The Appellant's own expert, however, admitted on cross-examination that roaches can be hazardous to health and that they can taint food with e-coli and salmonella if they walk across it. Trial Transcript at 40. Additionally, the evidence presented was that there were multiple live and dead roaches, fecal matter, exoskeletons and roach traps on the date of move in. This Court accepts the credibility assessments of the trial court as to the testimony of Mr. Tatge and Mr. Christophersen. The presence of cockroaches and their waste products to that degree is sufficient for the Court to conclude that the unit was unsanitary and therefore did not comply with the warranty of habitability according to the discussion of habitability set forth in Meese v. Fox. 200 N.W.2d 791, 796 (Iowa 1972). Therefore, the steps that the Appellee took to give notice and terminate her lease agreement were appropriate under Iowa Code section 562A.22.

CONCLUSION The Court adopts the trial court's findings and affirms the trial court's reasoning. Judgment is affirmed in favor of the Appellee in the amount of $2,010, plus interest at the rate of 4.4% per annum from the 22nd day of February, 2018, plus court costs. Attorney's fees were not requested and are therefore not granted. Clerk to notify.

Final Thoughts on the Christophersen Case

The attorney for Lillie Christophersen, Christopher Warnock, did not file a Satisfaction in Full on the case, meaning that the defendant, Apartments Downtown (Bryan Clark), didn't pay Lillie until March 8, 2019.

That means the legal ordeal for Lillie and her family went on for 582 days, or just over 1 year and 7 months, until Lillie got paid.

And even then, Lillie didn't recover attorney fees.

It's difficult to recover attorney fees at the small claims level. If you don't mention recovering attorney fees when filing your case, you're pretty much out of luck. Even if you do mention it, attorneys are expensive, and you can reach the limit of small claims court very quickly.

While attorneys can be involved at the small claims level, the point of small claims court was for individuals to work things out.

Bad landlords like Bryan Clark exploit this by employing an attorney as his registered agent, and then fighting everything – even the lawsuits where Clark and his gang of employee are clearly at-fault.

Don't lawsuits against bad landlords sound like fun?

Even with lawyers involved, lawsuits are protracted, complicated, expensive, and it takes forever to collect your money.

They're stressful.

Do you want to sign a lease with a bad landlord?

No, you don't.

I have more books planned about the Clarks and their obviously corrupt and illegal pattern of behavior towards good tenants and the law, and I'll talk more about that in the final chapter, The Rights of Good Tenants.

The Rights of Good Tenants

What have you learned from this short book?

You learned about the extremely messed up case with a bad landlord involving my friend and his daughter.

You learned about the bad landlord purposefully rips off good but ignorant tenants by accusation, theft, and abuse of the legal system.

You learned how most larger property management companies are set up as legal entities, and some of the people involved.

You learned how to search online databases through libraries or the courts to dig up dirt on potentially bad landlords.

You learned why lawsuits are a bad idea, and your friends and family's suggestions of filing a lawsuit are stupid.

You learned how the local media, police, housing authorities, activists, politicians, attorneys are completely worthless.

Will this book make a difference? I have no idea. This book covers a lot of topics. It's not just about bad landlords, being wary of signing leases, and why lawsuits are a bad idea. If you read this book and get interested in online research, that's a good thing.

I feel like this book, and the additional books I'll write on the Clarks, will help to chip away at their seemingly transparent existence and tell the stories of their systematic abuse of good tenants.

ABOUT THE AUTHOR

C. David Patterson is retired and splits his time between rural Warren County, Iowa, south of Des Moines, and hanging with his "LEO" buddies who live in The Ozarks in Southern Missouri.

This is his first book as C. David Patterson.